THINKING LOW

CAUSES AND IMPROVEMENT ON LOW SELF-ESTEEM

BY

CHRIS ADAM

TABLE OF CONTENTS

INTRODUCTION

Most people occasionally feel horrible about themselves. Being treated poorly by someone recently or in the past, as well as one's own evaluations of oneself, can all lead to feelings of low self-esteem. That is typical. But too many people live with poor self-esteem all the time, particularly those who struggle with mental health issues like depression, anxiety, phobias, psychosis, or delusional thinking. If you fall into this category, you might unnecessarily feel self-conscious throughout life. You are prevented from enjoying life, pursuing your interests, and achieving your goals if you have low self-esteem.

This book will provide you with suggestions on what you can do to improve your self-esteem and feel better about yourself. People like you who are working to raise their self-esteem and are aware of their poor self-esteem are the source of the ideas.

You could realize that you have some sensations of resistance to positive feelings about yourself when you start to employ the techniques in this booklet and additional strategies you may come up with to boost your self-esteem. That is typical. Don't let these emotions prevent you from having confidence in yourself. As you start to feel better and better about yourself, they will get smaller. Informing your pals of your struggles will help you feel better. If you can, let out a nice cry. Try relaxing activities like meditation or a warm bath.

Keep the following in mind while you read this booklet and perform the exercises:

"**I** am a very valuable, distinctive, and special individual. I should be proud of who I am."

CHAPTER ONE

MEANING OF LOW SELF-ESTEEM

When someone lacks confidence in who they are and what they can do, they have low self-esteem. They frequently feel unloved, unqualified, or inadequate. People who have trouble with low self-esteem are always worried about messing up or disappointing others.

Self-esteem problems can be harmful to your health and have a bad impact on your interpersonal and work connections. Your genes, your upbringing, your environment, and other factors all play a part in why you could have poor self-esteem.

However, your own mental health is a significant contributor to low self-esteem. Even when there is proof to the contrary, your inner voice or the thoughts in your head may constantly persuade you that you are insufficient or unworthy of anything. Low self-worth and low self-esteem are generally linked to negative thinking.

CHAPTER TWO

SIGNS OF LOW SELF-ESTEEM

A person's beliefs, feelings, and recurring patterns of behavior can all be impacted by low self-esteem. These indications may be more obvious at times, but they may also be much more subtly displayed.

Lack Of Control

Low self-esteem sufferers frequently feel powerless to change their circumstances or their life. This may be as a result of their perception that they are unable to significantly alter either their own lives or the external environment. Due to their external locus of control, people can believe they are helpless to make any changes to their difficulties.

According to my research, having a better sense of self-worth can help mitigate some of the negative consequences of situations when people have little control over what happens, which ultimately promotes mental health.
Finding techniques to raise your self-esteem may be beneficial for your wellbeing if you are having trouble not feeling like you have any control over your life or circumstance.

Poor Confidence

Poor self-esteem is more common among those with low self-confidence, and vice versa. You can depend on yourself to handle a variety of scenarios if you have faith in your ability and self-confidence.

Your general well-being may be greatly impacted by your ability to navigate the many diverse situations you may come across in life with this level of self-confidence.

This lack of confidence may be influenced by low self-esteem, but low confidence may also exacerbate or contribute to low self-esteem. It can be beneficial to learn how to boost your self-assurance and competence. One strategy you may use to increase your confidence and self-esteem is learning and practicing new abilities.

Negative Social Comparison

An individual's sense of self can occasionally be improved by social comparison. Though it can also have a negative impact on self-esteem, comparing yourself to others can be harmful. When comparing oneself to others, particularly those they perceive as superior to themselves, people with poor self-esteem may be more likely to engage in what is known as upward social comparison.

It's not necessarily negative to compare yourself to others who are doing better in society. These comparisons can occasionally provide insight and serve as a catalyst for development.

However, it can hinder self-esteem when people are left with emotions of inadequacy or despondency.
Social media might potentially be involved in these comparisons. Your

self-esteem can start to suffer if you often make negative comparisons to other users on social media platforms.

Problems Asking For What You Need

Low self-esteem might make it difficult for someone to ask for what they want. They could believe they are undeserving of assistance because of their low self-esteem. Having to ask for help and support could make them feel inadequate or embarrassed. They find it difficult to assert themselves when they are in need because they don't put their own needs first.

Despair And Self-doubt

Low self-worth individuals frequently fear that they made the wrong option even after making it. Instead of standing by their decisions, they frequently doubt their own judgment and give in to peer pressure.

People with low self-esteem may find it difficult to make decisions about their lives as a result of this, which frequently results in significant amounts of self-questioning and self-doubt.

Difficulty Accepting Good Comment

Low self-esteem is strongly associated to not being able to receive or make the most of praises from others, according to a 2017 study that was published in the Journal of Experimental Social Psychology.

People with poor self-esteem find it challenging to take compliments from others since they do not have a favorable opinion of themselves. Suspicion and mistrust are frequently expressed in response to this positive feedback. People with self-esteem problems may even think that the other person is being flippant or even harsh because these flattering statements do not match what they believe about themselves.

Negative Self-talk

People with low self-esteem tend to emphasize their weaknesses more so than their strengths. They constantly seem to have something terrible to say about themselves, instead of boosting their self-esteem with encouraging words. They always find fault with some aspect of themselves, whether it be their looks, demeanor, or skills, and they place the blame for everything going wrong on themselves.

Fear Of Success

People with poor self-esteem have self-doubt about their potential to succeed because they lack confidence in their skills. While they may be afraid of failing, they frequently shy away from difficulties or give up easily without giving it their all.

When things go wrong, lashing out or trying to find a means to cover feelings of inadequacy are just a few actions that can be attributed to this fear of failure. It's possible for people to offer defenses, place the responsibility on outside forces, or minimize the significance of the assignment.

Awful Prospects

People with low self-esteem also tend to believe that there are few chances for a better future. People with low self-esteem may find it difficult to adopt actions that would result in positive life changes due to these sentiments of hopelessness.

Another typical strategy for coping with these emotions is self-destructive behavior. People with low self-esteem are better able to find someone or something else to blame for what they perceive to be their own deficiencies by looking for challenges to success.

Lack Of Boundaries

It's common for boundaries to be set early in life. Children who have parents who respect and value them are more likely to be able to set healthy boundaries in adult relationships. Additionally, they are more likely to have a more favorable overall opinion of themselves.

Setting limits with other people might be challenging for persons who don't value themselves. If they strive to create or uphold a barrier, they could feel guilty or worry that people won't like them anymore.

When others disregard a person's time and space, this can lead to issues. A person may feel less valued as a result of the lack of respect in addition to stress.

An Attempt To Please Others

An additional typical sign of poor self-esteem is trying to please other people. When someone doesn't feel good about themselves, they may go above and beyond to make sure that others are at ease and content in order to receive external reinforcement. This frequently entails putting other people's needs above their own, saying yes to things they might not want to do, and feeling bad for declining.

CHAPTER THREE

IMPACT OF LOW SELF-ESTEEM

Having low self-esteem might make it more challenging to accomplish your goals and build supportive, healthy relationships. Additionally, certain mental health issues and diseases, such as anxiety and depression, may be influenced by it.

Low self-esteem has also been linked to a higher likelihood of suicide thoughts, according to research.

People with low self-esteem may also be more vulnerable to criticism or rejection. Negative criticism might be harder to ignore for someone with low self-worth than for someone with strong self-esteem, who is more likely to be able to brush it aside. This may also increase the likelihood that individuals with low self-esteem would give up when presented with difficulties or hurdles.

It has been discovered through research that individuals with low self-esteem frequently exhibit actions that serve to protect their frail sense of value. In an effort to win others' support, behaviors like seeming depressed or pouting are used.

Sadly, these actions frequently have negative effects. They wind up eliciting unfavorable responses from other people instead of receiving the assistance and encouragement they require to raise their self-esteem.

CHAPTER FOUR

COPING WITH LOW SELF-ESTEEM

Having low self-esteem can have a negative impact on your emotional health, so it's critical to take action to improve your self-worth and seek the assistance you require. Although it takes time to increase your self-esteem, there are things you can do to safeguard your mental health in the interim. You could try the following things, which could be helpful:

Focus On Hopeful Thoughts

Focus on thinking uplifting, hopeful things for a short while each day. Recognize your small strengths and give yourself permission to be proud of them. Even though you might not be feeling your best right now, you have the power and stamina to go through it. Just think back to instances in the past when you overcame extremely challenging situations.

Care For Yourself

You may occasionally feel as though you are unworthy of kindness and consideration if you have low self-esteem. Find ways to show yourself kindness, no matter how small, by keeping in mind that you need to be taken care of. Time should be spent engaging in enjoyable activities. Permit some downtime for yourself.

It Is vitally essential for both your physical and emotional health to make an investment in your own comfort and care. This is not a luxury or something you should earn.

Get Some Outside Support

Talk to a friend who can support you no matter what you are going through. In addition to being a friend or family member, this could also be a professional like a doctor, therapist, teacher, or clergy member.

It can be beneficial while you attempt to raise your self-esteem to have a network of kind individuals who value you and want you to value yourself.

CHAPTER FIVE

HOW TO BUILD SELF-ESTEEM

There are things you may do to help you feel better about yourself if you are having self-esteem issues. These tactics include, among others:

Be Aware of Your Thoughts

Start observing the default negative ideas you experience each day. It's critical to actively identify cognitive fallacies and swap out negative thinking for constructive thinking when negative thoughts start to take hold.

Absolve Yourself

It's critical to develop self-forgiveness and the ability to get past your shortcomings and mistakes if you have a tendency to dwell on them. By doing this, you may take your attention away from the bad things that have happened in the past and instead keep it on the things you can do better in the future.

Develop Self Acceptance

It's critical to let go of the notion that to be valuable, you must be flawless. Work on embracing who you are right now. This is not to say that you don't have objectives or things you might want to work on altering, but it's critical to understand that you are deserving of respect and love both from yourself and from others just the way you are at this very moment

Honor Your Self

Consider the accomplishments and qualities in which you take pride for some time. Without making comparisons or concentrating on things you'd like to alter, allow yourself to appreciate your worth and your talents.

Even if you don't have to improve to value yourself, doing so can help you achieve your objectives.

To think of yourself as you would a friend can be beneficial. How would you respond if a loved one was in the same predicament? It's likely that you would often show them love, patience, understanding, and understanding instead of criticizing them, so it's crucial to do the same for yourself.

CHAPTER SIX

OTHER WAYS TO INCREASE LOW SELF-ESTEEM

Here are some pointers for increasing your self-esteem

Make Physical Health Improvements

Being in shape and healthy makes it much simpler to feel good about ourselves.

As a result of their perception that they don't "deserve" to be taken care of, people with low self-esteem frequently ignore their own needs.

Consider increasing your exercise, healthy food, and sleep duration. Making time for relaxation and doing what you want to do rather than what other people want of you is another smart move. You might discover that small adjustments like this have a big impact on how you feel about life in general.

Give Yourself A Break

You don't need to be flawless all the time. Even having a positive self-image is optional.

Self-esteem varies from circumstance to circumstance, from day to day, and hour to hour. When around friends and coworkers, some people seem at ease and optimistic, but when with strangers, they are uncomfortable and reserved. Others could suffer socially even when they feel completely in control of themselves at work (or vice versa).

Give yourself a break. Everyone experiences periods of feeling a little depressed or having difficulty maintaining their self-belief.

The secret is to not be too harsh on yourself. Don't be too harsh on yourself and try to be gentle to yourself. By rewarding yourself, you can improve your sense of self-worth .

Gain More Self-Assurance And The Ability To Say No

The ability to defend oneself or refuse requests from others is frequently difficult for those who have poor self-esteem.

Since they don't like to turn anyone away, they could end up being overworked at home or at work. This, however, might make stress worse and more difficult to control.

You can raise your self-esteem by practicing assertiveness. You can sometimes boost your self-confidence by acting as though you believe in yourself!

CHAPTER SEVEN

CONCLUSION

Your capacity to pursue objectives, create healthy relationships, and feel positive about yourself all depend heavily on your level of self-esteem. While everyone occasionally struggles with their confidence, low self-esteem can negatively impact your ability to feel happy and may even increase your risk of developing mental health issues like anxiety and depression.

There are ways to obtain assistance if you are showing signs of low self-esteem. Think about consulting a physician or other mental health expert. Your low self-esteem can be improved and your confidence and opinion of yourself and your skills can be raised by working with a therapist to modify the cognitive patterns that contribute to it.

Even though it could take some time and work to change your perspective of yourself, you can eventually learn to better accept and value who you are.

www.ingramcontent.com/pod-product-compliance
Lightning Source LLC
LaVergne TN
LVHW020537160826
845677LV00015B/4117

* 9 7 9 8 8 4 7 7 2 9 8 4 0 *